Working like a DOG

An amusing handbook for managers who relate to dogs

PATRICIA MAY JULLIAN

Copyright © 2014 Patricia May Jullian
All rights reserved.
ISBN: 1490927158
ISBN 13: 9781490927152
Library of Congress Control Number: 2013913117
CreateSpace Independent Publishing Platform
North Charleson, South Carolina

Working like a Dog

written and illustrated by
PATRICIA MAY JULLIAN

Dedicated to my mom who believed that I could accomplish anything, and my husband who gave me enough space to do so and of course all the dogs I have owned and loved: Mollee, Bristle, Shadow, Sheba, Murphy, Saki, Mate and Bandee

Table of Contents

Introduction ix

Section One: Dogs and their Human Counterparts

The Australian Shepherd 2
The Beagle 4
The Chow Chow 6
The Jack Russell Terrier 8
The Labrador Retriever 10
The Poodle 12
The German Shepherd 14
The Teacup 16
The Rottweiler 18

Section Two: Tips for the Leader of the Pack

The Interview 23
Put the Dog in the Right Home and the Employee in the Right Job 26
Accountability and Compliments 28
Don't bite the Hand That Feeds You 30
Let's Play Fetch (A Poor Action Plan) 32
The Alpha Dog as the Boss 34
The Alpha Dog as an Employee 37
Pack Qualities 39
Treating Everyone Fairly Doesn't Mean Treating Everyone the Same 41
The Wolf in Sheep's Clothing 42
The Wolf in Sheep's Clothing in Leadership 44
The Best Day at Work 45

Not the Best Day at Work 46
Bad Doggie 48
Praise, Praise, Praise 50
Evaluations 51
Pure Breeds, Mixed Breeds, and Training 52
What Breed of Dog are You? 54
What Breed of Dog Do You Own? 55
What Breed of Dog is the Author? 56

Introduction

Being a boss is one of the hardest things that I have ever done. One day I was Alice and the next day I had fallen through the rabbit hole into another reality. People looked at me differently. All of a sudden, I was supposed to know everything—as if my X chromosome had suddenly mutated.

People who'd known me as a co-worker thought that they would not have any rules once I fell down the hole. But I was always a good worker, an overachiever, and followed the rules. So why wouldn't I continue that mind-set when I became a supervisor and then a director? Other people, upon meeting me, tried to size me up. They had to learn not to confuse kindness with weakness.

It is my job to make every employee successful. It is the right thing to do. I don't do it for thanks or rewards; in fact, I expect the opposite. Although many employees have thanked me for giving them guidance, writing letters of recommendation for school, finding them internships, standing up for them, and lending a listening ear, others feel entitled. They act as though they are my only employee and deserve special treatment. A few years ago, a human-resources representative called me and said that one of my employees had complained that my evaluations were unfair and she deserved a better raise. This employee had been sentenced to jail time for driving under the influence of alcohol or drugs, and I had cooperated with the department of corrections so she could work while she served her sentence. I also let her pick up extra shifts during this time. The HR representative told me to get a pen and paper and write down, "No good deed goes unpunished." Over the years, I have referred to that paper more than once.

Work is called work because that is exactly what it is. Otherwise, we would go to play every day. The principal thing I have learned is that most employees do not remember what you have done for them. They constantly wonder, "What has my boss done for me *lately*?"

Having been an overly sensitive person for my entire life, I have found that the best way to cope with negative behavior is to try to figure out why people do the things that they do. If I can understand why people act the way they do, I will not take their actions personally. That makes me a better boss, better able to support them.

My mom taught me to try to find something good in everyone. She maintained that the more people I liked, the happier I would be. That bit of advice worked for me while I was growing up and while I raised my children as a single parent. If my co-workers were not getting along, I would just mind my own business and do my own work. I did not get involved.

Good bosses have to get involved, however. A toxic employee will drive the good employees away. The boss has to prevent that. Now, since I am living the dream of being a leader, I have to be the peacemaker. I have to look at each side of a conflict and encourage people to get along. I try to believe that people truly want to do their best at work, although their behavior sometimes gets in the way.

There is a saying, "The more I know people, the more I love my dog." After being bitten by a few employees—and trying to protect myself from the barks and bites of others—it became very clear to me that I had to be the alpha female. It was my job to help everyone succeed but not at my own expense. I had to figure out what they needed but set boundaries at the same time.

In addition to being the alpha female, I found that having a great sense of humor would get me through most situations. Just when I think that our department is doing well and everyone is pulling his or her weight and performing his or her job, someone will do something that I didn't expect. Here are some of my favorite surprises. I walked over to an employee's work area to talk to him. He wasn't there, but the following message, on a sticky note, was. "Thanks for everything you have done for me, but I quit." Another time, an employee called to say he wouldn't be in because he had to do yard work. I understand taking time off when the employee is ill, his child is ill, or even the dog is ill. But yard work? No.

One day while trying to figure out the best way to deal with a couple of employees who were not getting along—one was snarling and the other was nipping in defense—I decided that categorizing them by dog breeds, according to my interpretations, helped me to figure out how to handle them. It also enable me to retain my alpha female position, protect myself, and maintain my sense of humor. We compare humans to dogs in our everyday conversation, so this is not a new concept. Saying, "He is a dog," means something very different from saying, "She is a dog." "He is in the doghouse" and "I wouldn't treat a dog like that" are other comparisons. Then there are the "dog days of August." It is common wisdom that "you can't teach an old dog new tricks" and you should "let sleeping dogs lie." Dog-breed categories reflect personalities and the way the animals approach work, rather than physical characteristics.

To develop your team, you must look at both the type of business you have and the customers you serve. You don't want poodles working as guard dogs or German shepherds working in a beauty parlor. This doesn't mean that all of your employees must be alike, but they all must understand the common goals and culture of the business. If your company's mission statement is something like,

"We provide excellent customer service regardless of race, color, or creed every day in a professional manner without hesitation, blah blah blah," as most mission statements go, employees may not relate to it or remember it. Short and sweet works. "The customer is always right." "It's all about the patient." Sit, stay, shake. Be direct and to the point.

The dog breeds that I describe in this book are similar to people who may be working with you. Just like employees, no breed is bad; you just need to know what motivates them and what their personality is like. You need to have the correct breed performing the correct task.

SECTION ONE:
Dogs and their Human Counterparts

THE AUSTRALIAN SHEPHERD

Traits of the Breed

The Australian shepherd is a working dog. She needs jobs to do or she will find things to do that may not be in her—or your—best interest, such as chewing up your sofa pillows. She is highly intelligent. She understands hand signals and directions but she needs guidance. She gets bored easily. She not only has a lot of energy but she likes to keep others on the move. She was bred to round up livestock.

Traits of the Employee

This employee is a hard worker and will abide by the rules as long as she knows them. If she finds extra time, she may go outside of her job description and find things to do that may get her or the company into trouble. Her intentions are always good, but she might not understand boundaries. This type of employee might order paper for the department from a company that is not under contract. She was only trying to help, and it appeared that the new company provided cheaper paper. By the way, buying paper wasn't even in her job description.

Leash

Yes, for both the breed and the employee. The dog may nip the letter carrier in the heels in an effort to get him to go in the right direction. Likewise, the employee needs the leash or she will have a tendency to wander about the department getting into trouble.

To Make Her Successful

Keep her busy; put her in charge of an area or a workflow. She is smart, a critical thinker, and will be a great asset to any company. But she needs to know the boundaries. Even though she excels at doing routine things, she needs extra assignments and praise or she will get bored and feel unappreciated. Keep her close to you and know what she is doing. She is a hard worker and would do well as a motivational speaker. She can easily herd people into her way of thinking.

THE BEAGLE

Traits of the Breed
The beagle has a keen sense of smell and is good at hunting rabbits and other small game. Once she has picked up a scent, it may be hard to call her back, as she will become stubborn. In other aspects, she is obedient and likes to be a member of the pack. She loves to bark and howl.

Traits of the Employee
Overall, she is a good employee but she is very sensitive to perfumes in the workplace. She will complain loudly about being allergic to scents and smells. Once she has started a task, she wants to finish it—even if other, more important tasks surface. She likes to sniff things out. She likes to get to the bottom of an issue but may become so focused on one issue that she lets other things slide.

Leash
In the wild, outside of work, this dog does not need a leash. But in the workplace, she needs guidance and deadlines. The deadline is her leash and will make her focus.

To Make Her Successful
Give this employee a short list of tasks. She will tend to pour herself into getting the tasks completed but may not prioritize or know when the task is actually finished. She needs guidance and cannot be in a work environment without supervision. She requires deadlines and limitations. She will excel in a position where she can work on one thing at a time. She would make a great mystery writer or research scientist.

THE CHOW CHOW

Traits of the Breed
This breed is similar to a cat. She demands attention and can be very jealous. She is stubborn and likes to be in the center of everything. The breed has been known to bite and is protective of both owners and property. She requires an alpha master.

Traits of the Employee
This employee is a great worker but she also loves to socialize. She has a tendency to go from person to person to relay a personal problem that she is having or to complain about another employee. She cannot be alone with her thoughts. She must express them repeatedly and get input from her co-workers. At her best, she is friendly and amusing and she can bring people together. At her worst, she gossips incessantly, causing problems among co-workers and between the staff and management. The dilemma is that she is great at her job except for the gossiping. She has a tendency to go behind the boss's back. Instead of stabbing the boss in the back, she bites the boss in the back. She doesn't like criticism and finds it threatening. If she becomes a manager, she will defend her staff and department. She thinks she is always right and will snap at others as a defensive mechanism before she will listen to the whole story.

Leash
Since she has a high energy level, it would be best to keep her on a leash. Containing her is hard. A bark collar would be an excellent way to keep her quiet. But this would not sit well with the HR department.

To Make Her Successful
Use her as an ally. Have her champion a cause. It must be something that is near and dear to her heart or she will undermine you. She is hard to control but will always try to do her best. She can be a huge distraction in the workplace, so she needs mentoring and guidance to stay on track. Praise her for her excellent work and teach her that gossiping is destructive to the work environment. She has a tendency to think that management is out to get everyone. She needs to be monitored constantly and be taught to be accountable. If she is in management, she will be hard to control.

THE JACK RUSSELL TERRIER

Traits of the Breed
This dog is highly energetic and requires exercise and stimulation. She loves to learn tricks and then perform them for her owner, a guest, or anyone who will give her attention. She is highly intelligent. She is not the type of dog to be left alone in an apartment all day long. Eddie on the TV show *Frasier* is a Jack Russell, so being an actress is not outside her realm.

Traits of the Employee
She likes to be the center of attention. She can be very entertaining and amusing. She loves people but loves their full attention even more. She was probably the class clown in school and she may have not matured beyond that level. She would make a great public speaker if only she could stay on track. She enjoys multitasking and running from one task to another, as she gets bored easily. At her best, she accomplishes a lot of work. At her worst, she is just entertaining.

Leash
Lots of luck trying to put a leash on her. She is busy; she has things to do. So you may have a hard time catching her.

To Make Her Successful
She needs to be in a job that does not require sitting at a desk all day. She needs to work with her hands or to be involved in work that keeps her moving physically. She can move mountains when she wants to but she will have to stop and chat. Remember that she needs acknowledgment. You must show her that you appreciate her and give her lots of treats, as she is probably one of your best workers. She would be a great public speaker or life coach.

THE LABRADOR RETRIEVER

Traits of the Breed

The Labrador has a good temperament and is easygoing and trusting with strangers, so she doesn't make a good guard dog. She is kind, pleasant, and even-tempered. She is not noisy or territorial. She makes a great assistance dog and can be trained to be a guide dog or a rescue dog.

Traits of the Employee

This employee is one of your stars. She gets along with everyone. She enjoys her job and rarely complains. Although she has the aptitude for doing many jobs, she is happy in her current position. It is wise to have someone like her as your receptionist, since she will set the tone for the whole department. When outside customers call or arrive at her desk, you can count on her to greet them happily.

Leash

No leash is required; she can be counted on to stay by your side.

To Make Her Successful

Continue to mentor her to help her move up the corporate ladder, but she is probably happy right where she is. Realize that she may be your mentor, as she can balance work and home life. To continue her success, make sure that you never take her for granted and continue to thank her. If she gets into management, she has to be careful to stick to the rules and not try to please everyone. Because she tries to make everyone happy and is patient, she would make a great teacher or nurse.

THE POODLE

Traits of the Breed
The standard Poodle is highly intelligent and trainable. She is good-natured, graceful, and proud. She is usually calm but can become high strung if she does not get the proper amount of exercise. Her owner must be firm but loving, as this dog will not respond to harshness. She dislikes being alone. She requires extensive grooming.

Traits of the Employee
This employee is intelligent and a good worker. She can appear to be aloof or stuck up at times. She is an alpha female and may not even acknowledge someone she thinks is not as strong as she is. On the surface, she appears to be a show dog. She is a fashion diva, wears heels and a lot of bling, and stands out in a crowd. She may have an insecurity that she hides with all of this fluff. Underneath the fluff, she can be a devoted and loyal friend and employee, but it will take some time to earn her trust. Other employees may not take the time to work through the barriers that she can put up.

Leash
This employee would love a rhinestone leash. Actually, diamonds would be more to her liking, since she likes to stand out. Grooming is highly important to her. She may spend some of her time checking out other people's outfits to see if they meet her high standards.

To Make Her Successful
She needs firm, not harsh guidance. She needs to know that she is doing a good job and is appreciated. Let her know that you appreciate her fashion sense as well, as there is some type of insecurity here or she wouldn't have the need to prance about and distinguish herself from others. She sets high standards for her friends, so some of her co-workers may find her critical and unapproachable. You must remember that she will always do her best and that she has a kind heart. These traits must be brought to the forefront. She would make an excellent salesperson or liaison for the company.

THE GERMAN SHEPHERD

Traits of the Breed

The German shepherd was bred for her intelligence. She is an excellent guard dog and can be territorial. She not only likes rules, but she wants everyone else to follow them as well. A friend's German shepherd gets upset if people or dogs are roughhousing. She is much happier when everyone has a place and is in her place. German shepherds are called police dogs for a very good reason.

Traits of the Employee

This employee is intelligent and a great worker but will complain if co-workers deviate from the rules. She likes everything to be perfect or she gets upset. German shepherds make great supervisors or quality assurance managers.

Leash

If she is put on a leash, she wants to be the one doing the leading.

To Make Her Successful

She needs rules and wants them to be followed. If she is not in a management position, she probably needs to be as that is how she thinks. She would make an excellent supervisor, police officer, accountant, HR representative, or quality control coordinator.

THE TEACUP

Traits of the Breed
This is not actually a breed but is any small dog that can fit in a cup, or a purse and be carried around and told how cute she is.

Traits of the Employee
This employee won't stay with the company long as she wants to be arm candy. Unfortunately, her self-esteem may be low so she feels better being told that she is pretty. She has always been pretty and didn't learn how to develop her inner qualities. Not all pretty women are like this but this breed is.

Leash
This employee doesn't require a leash but a container.

To Make Her Successful
A real teacup employee will probably have a hard time finding a job that she likes unless it is modeling. She will make a great trophy wife. To make her successful bring out her inner worth and abilities. You may be the first person who has taken the time to do this so be patient.

THE ROTTWEILER

Traits of the Breed
Although very loyal and courageous, this breed can be trained to be vicious. She can be hard to train, as she thinks that she is in charge of the household. While training her, you must be firm but kind.

Traits of the Employee
This employee can be very loyal and will stand up for what she believes in, but do not cross her. She has to be correct. She will hold grudges and go after anyone she thinks might undermine her.

Leash
This employee may be very hard to lead, and a leash will not help. If this employee gets into a management position and you must work with her, keep her at a distance. She is very hard to deal with.

To Make Her Successful
It would be best if this employee were successful at someone else's establishment. But if she reports to you, set firm rules. Expect her to be stubborn and headstrong. She will correct someone during a meeting if he mispronounces a word, states the incorrect date, or isn't perfect. It doesn't matter who the person is, as this employee is extremely critical and derives security from perfection as she defines it.

SECTION TWO:
Tips for the Leader of the Pack

The Interview

Do you like the culture you have in your department or do you want to change it? If you are opening a new business, you can decide what culture you would like to have and make that your priority while hiring people. It is very hard to get to know a potential employee during a one-hour interview so your questions not only have to uncover technical skills but dig deeper to see what type of person you are hiring. Keep in mind that your best technical employee who has a high energy level, like a Jack Russell terrier, may require extra jobs to keep her busy. Your German shepherds may be great at quality assurance but may not be able to warm up to customers. I have always asked my interviewees who their mentors were in life but now I also ask, "If you were a dog, what breed would you be and why?" That question gives me even better insight.

Hiring an employee, even with the interview and background check that must be done, is much easier than firing an employee. It is best to hire applicants whom other employees recommend, but even then, you have to be careful. People don't always see weaknesses that their friends may possess in the workplace. You might ask behavioral questions, such as, "How do you typically deal with conflict and give an example?" since these responses usually provide a good insight into an applicant's basic personality, but some people are very good at interviews. I once had someone show up in my office with a suitcase to give the impression that she had flown in for the interview—the job was that important to her. She did live about forty miles from the job location but she didn't fly in for the interview. If only she had put that much thought and inspiration into her work, she would still be working for me.

Yes, I was fooled. This traveling employee had a great interview. She was very personable and told a good story. Looking back, I probably would have hired her again based on that interview. Her performance was less than stellar, however. She spent a lot of her time talking to people from other departments. Sometimes she actually hid from work. She was highly entertaining and friendly, so people liked her. But the people who worked with her got tired of picking up the slack. There is probably a good job for her out there somewhere if she could work when she felt like it, do whatever she pleased, and get reinforcement for her funny remarks. In the dog world, a "teacup" breed gets to visit places while being carried. No effort is required of her, yet she gets praise for being cute and being dressed in adorable outfits. The employee who fooled me would make a great teacup dog.

While interviewing potential employees, I ask them who their mentor has been in life and why. When the answer is "my father because he was such a hard worker, he never missed a day of work, he was always on time, and consistently did the right thing," it is usually true that the candidate also holds these values. When a candidate lists a pop singer or a sports figure "because he makes a lot of money and gets to buy a lot of things," I know that this person feels entitled. I don't need her on my staff. When an employee either doesn't know what a mentor is or can't think of any, I am concerned. The interview process can be stressful, so I will study her responses to the rest of my questions before I make my decision.

Our first mentors are our parents; they teach us how to take care of ourselves. But most people have many mentors during their lives. We only realize it if we take the time to look back and examine our lives. Then we discover who has helped to guide us down our path.

Put the Dog in the Right Home and the Employee in the Right Job

Dogs have the need to please and are happy when they are getting praise from their owners. Most employees want to do a good job and enjoy praise in the form of a raise, a thank you, and acknowledgment. The employees who don't care, don't show up, or hide to avoid working normally don't stay employed for long. Those are not the employees with whom you will be working, since they will probably not stay with the company. These people can be very personable and have great interview skills, so occasionally you will be tricked and bring one on board. They aren't bad people but they have an aversion to work in general or they are not in the right job. It's like trying to teach a retriever to herd sheep. A border collie has the innate ability to herd, but if you try to teach her to retrieve game, you both will get frustrated.

It is very important to get the right people into the right professions and doing the tasks that best suit their personalities. The problem is that many people fall into a job and stay there because they are comfortable, not because they are living their passion. The employees that you will be working with really want to be successful but may have barriers that keep them from maximizing their potential. Part of being a mentoring boss is to find out what the barriers are and to remove or reduce them.

Employees need to take ownership, reflect on their job, and see if they are in the right position. Too many people settle for a job instead of furthering their education and getting into a line of work they enjoy. They may have a fear of failure and need to have their abilities pointed out to them.

Accountability and Compliments

Accountability is an area where employees and dogs are alike. Certain responses should be taught in school, such as taking responsibility and knowing how to accept a compliment. These are two sides of the same coin. For some people, the correct response comes naturally. Others must learn it.

If you perform a job incorrectly and your manager speaks to you about it, the best way to show that you are a responsible employee is to acknowledge the error and learn from it. It is never a good boss's intention to beat up an employee over an error, and the employee should not beat up herself. We all have to learn from the error, put safeguards in place so it won't happen again, and move on.

The same is true for dogs. You can find your dog sitting in a pile of feathers, with one hanging from her mouth, and a torn pillow at her feet, and she will look at you as if to say, "I don't know what happened. I walked into the room and discovered it in disarray." She has to learn, what "no" means, which toys are hers, and what she is not allowed to touch. If she isn't trained, she will repeat the bad behavior.

For employees, it's helpful to have written procedures so that a worker may review them to see how she is supposed to handle a work-flow. The written procedure is not just for her use; you can also refer to the accepted method if it needs to be explained in a court of law or to a regulatory agency. The procedure sets up expectations. Because it is written, it will not change unless you want to change it. The employee needs to be given competency tests, as well. The workplace is always changing and we must train and retrain our employees to make them successful. Don't assume that simply giving updates to employees is sufficient notice of a change or how it will affect them. Change needs to be a constant conversation. The boss must use competency tests in a way that is educational and not threatening. To be our most effective, we all need to see where we need to improve.

When it comes to accepting a compliment, people and dogs differ. People can have trouble accepting compliments. Some tend to brush them off or put themselves down, which makes the person who gave the compliment regret that she said anything. On the surface, an employee may be embarrassed to receive the compliment but she probably does like to know that she is appreciated.

Teach employees that when they receive a compliment, all they have to do is smile and say thank you. That's it. They don't have to downgrade the compliment. They don't have to think, "I am not worthy." I had a chemistry professor who taught me how to take a compliment, and I have passed that on to people with whom I have worked. Our canine companions know how to take a compliment; we can learn from them. They just cock their heads to one side, give that little doggy smile, and wag their tails. Both owner and dog are happy.

Don't bite the Hand That Feeds You

Dogs form an alliance with the person who feeds them and takes care of them. They trust that person, follow him around, and protect him. Employees are not usually like this. Generation Y workers (born from the 1980s to the 1990s) want daily feedback and are more loyal to their team than their employer. Some employees will jump from one job to another for a fifty-cent-an-hour increase. They have no loyalty. They live in the moment. They would rather have money in their pockets than have medical insurance. They don't think about tomorrow; they live for today. Pensions and retirement are so far away that you might as well be speaking another language when you mention them. You cannot entice these workers with these benefits. They need to know what hours they will be working, since they would like to have their jobs wrap around their personal lives. They will use vacation time as soon as they get it, not worrying about what will happen if they get sick and need time off in the future. They will do a good job while at work, but work does not come first in their lives.

Actually, our society has helped to change the loyalty factor. Before we were such a mobile society, an employee would stay with one company until he retired. Over the years, companies have downsized, laid off employees, and transferred employees away from their families to the opposite side of the country. Loyalty goes both ways. If we want loyal employees, we must be loyal to them as well. Large, faceless, emotionless companies that tend to see employees as numbers and judge them by how much they can produce have replaced the mom-and-pop businesses. "It is not personal, it is business" is the phrase now used. We can't really blame our employees for looking out for themselves, since no one else will.

But it can't just be about the bottom line. We need to appreciate what our employees can do for the company. Four high-achieving employees who work well together can accomplish much more than ten moderately high-achieving employees who bicker and don't really want to be on the job.

Let's Play Fetch
(A Poor Action Plan)

A friend recently conveyed a story about her grandmother trying to teach her dog how to fetch a ball. She picked up a ball and threw it across the room. Then she picked up the dog and placed the dog right next to the ball. She then picked up the ball again and threw it to the other side of the room. The dog stayed where she had been placed, so the woman picked her up, carried her across the room, and placed her next to the ball again. Needless to say, the dog did not learn how to fetch. What the dog did learn was to sit, watch the woman throw the ball across the room, wait, get a free ride across the room to the ball, wait again, watch the ball, and get another free ride across the room. It was great fun with little energy required.

We make the same mistake with our employees. When we are working with an underachiever or an employee with a behavioral issue, we must first give them an action plan so they understand the expected behavior. We cannot do everything for them; they must take the action. The action plan must list either the specific desired behaviors or the specific undesired behaviors and what actions are needed to achieve the desired behaviors. The behaviors must be measurable so the employee can receive valid feedback. Most employees can exhibit the desired behavior with coaching. Some employees would rather sit and watch someone else throw the ball across the room. They don't really care if they have the job or not.

I felt terrible the first time that I had to write someone up for excessive absences. The employee wasn't fazed at all. Later, in a management class, I learned that it may be hard for a manager to discipline an employee, but the counseling session that the manager has with the employee is unlikely to be the employee's first experience of that sort. The employee may have been a regular in the principal's office since kindergarten. She is used to being counseled. Some even like it because they are getting attention. When you start working harder to save your employee's job than she is, you need to let go. You are carrying her to the ball. Cut your losses and hire someone who really wants the job and fits in with the rest of the employees and the tasks that need to be done.

The Alpha Dog as the Boss

Ask yourself if you deserve to be the alpha dog. In the past, people would respect the titles supervisor, director, and manager. Today, however, you must prove yourself to your employees. It is not enough that you have advanced degrees or have been in the field for thirty years. Younger employees with no experience and less education would like your job. Your hours appear to be better; you spend a lot of time at your desk (they assume that you are answering your e-mail, surfing the Internet, or shopping on eBay or Craigslist); and they know that you earn more than they do. They don't know or care that you are responsible for every penny spent by the department; you are responsible for all of the work that they put out, good or bad; or that you must make sure that all regulations are being followed. You make sure that their check is correct and that their needs are met. You help them obtain FMLA (Family and Medical Leave Act) if needed. Basically, you make sure that management and co-workers treat them fairly. After all, they are your puppies.

For employees to accept that you are the alpha dog, they must trust you. They must trust that you will treat everyone fairly. The best way to do this is to let everyone know the rules and to enforce them. If the rule is that an employee gets a written warning after five absences, then make sure to give one after five absences. The staff must understand that an absence is an absence. If an employee is not at work doing her job when scheduled, she is absent. Period. Depending on your company's policies, absences may be counted differently. For example, a stay in the hospital may count as one absence, but it is still an absence. If you have a policy of no excused absences except for jury duty or approved FMLA, you do not have to decide which absences are valid and which are not. I have received notes from doctors, faxes from the fire department, and phone calls from spouses to get an employee's absence excused. My thought is that if you didn't come to work, you may have had a valid reason but you were still absent.

As a manager, you must protect all of your employees. If you counsel an employee for absences, you cannot tell the other employees that you counseled that employee. Most times, the offender's co-workers do not know that she has been counseled, so they assume that she is getting away with bad behavior. It is frustrating that they think this, but you have to pat yourself on the back because you did your job. You are dealing with the issue but still protecting the employee.

A word of caution here: Perception and reality are not the same things. The employee's perception of reality is what matters. I had a boss who had a meeting which was out of the office every Wednesday afternoon, but when clients called to talk with her, her secretary said she played golf every Wednesday afternoon. No one knows where the secretary received that information. She didn't make it up. Perhaps she heard part of a conversation and thought that the boss played golf every Wednesday afternoon. Most perceptions develop lives of their own, and the boss never finds out about them. In the golf case, a client informed the boss what the secretary told him so that the boss could change her secretary's perception and behavior.

There are so many rules and regulations in a company to keep everyone safe and protected that it is understandable that employees sometimes get confused. Even if you review expectations and the reasons for them, misperceptions will still exist. Remember that the employee sees the world from her own viewpoint. I didn't realize that my clothes didn't wash and iron themselves until I left home. If all employees experienced being boss, their perceptions would change. But by the time one of your employees reaches the level of being a boss, you will be off at another job or retired, so you will never see that growth. Most don't want to have the title of boss but would rather simply criticize their current boss. Because we live in a litigious society, a smart manager lets her HR representative know when she has a problem employee. Because HR has to represent the employee and the employer, it will take a long time to work a troublesome employee out of the organization. Be patient, be persistent, and be factual. Log dates and times that counseling sessions were held after infractions. Record the consequences of the employee's actions, too. Did other employees have to work overtime to compensate? Did the company lose a customer? Was a patient unhappy with the service she received? If your company uses verbal, written, and final written warnings, use the process. HR will not back you if you don't document the steps you take and follow the procedures that are in place.

The Alpha Dog as an Employee

Although there may be a reporting structure in your company, there is probably only one boss over a department or area. The boss is the alpha male or female. In the canine world, the strongest dog is the alpha. After a fight or two, the pack knows who the alpha is. The alpha is the first one in the pack to eat; the other pack members respect the alpha. There are rules and a social structure within the pack.

In the work force, the pack works differently. Some employees resist authority. Although the company or department should be open to new ideas, some suggestions conflict with safety factors or regulations. Some employees do not see or care to see the big picture. They do not want to learn the regulations or how the company actually runs. These employees will dislike a manager just because she is the manager. It may not be evident to the employee that she dislikes authority figures—she may not be at this level in her development—but she will voice her opinions to other employees, complaining that the boss doesn't understand the workload, doesn't know how to schedule, or doesn't discipline the "bad employees." The boss can't tolerate this behavior. It undermines the department or company. Usually this behavior is covert. The boss doesn't discover it until another employee complains about it. At that point, the boss must tell the employee who resists authority that her behavior is disruptive to the department.

If there is a specific issue, such as why a change cannot be implemented, the boss should discuss it as well so the coaching session can be a learning opportunity for this employee.

Don't be surprised if this behavior continues. There will always be an employee or two who will try to undermine you. Usually, these are high-performing employees who have a lot of clout with the other employees, and this is why they are so dangerous. Once you have coached this employee and let her know that her behavior is unacceptable, it may become even more covert. Eventually this person may leave the company. But she will do as much damage as she can before she does. And you may hear from her again. She will be one of the people who applies for a job within a year of leaving because she doesn't like the manager at her new job. Don't believe her covert complaining trait has changed and don't take her back.

Even though the boss is the alpha female, she shouldn't have received the position because she is an outspoken tyrant. She should have gotten the position because she sees the whole picture, is intelligent, and truly cares about the potential of each employee. The employees who try to undermine her do not possess these traits but they are outspoken and leaders in their own right, as they get people to listen to them. Let them lead elsewhere. You don't need their disruptions.

Pack Qualities

The staff exhibits pack-like qualities. They watch each other for weakness and attack. Employee attacks are a little more subtle than the canine variety—they don't snarl, bite, and scratch—but their attacks can be as deadly. Usually the attack is covert. They exclude a person and talk to others about her. When things are going well, the staff will work as a team. They get along and get a lot of work done. If a team member is going through a hard time in her life and her work is sliding, the rest of the team senses that she has become weak. Canine packs physically attack the weakest dog. In a human pack, the individual members will exclude the weak member, gossip about her, and finally go to management to complain about her.

An employee once told me in confidence that she had Hodgkin's disease but would continue to work during her treatments. All the staff knew was that Susie started to wear wigs and frequently called in sick. The staff became very critical of her appearance and thought that she wasn't doing her share of the work. Since she had told me about her condition in confidence, I could not share that information with the complainers. I could hint that maybe something was going on with her and that they should be compassionate. If they had known the nature of the problem, they would have made allowances for her. People need to give each other the benefit of the doubt without having to know the whole story. That is true compassion.

Many times, when a good employee starts to struggle, I will invite her into my office and ask if there is something I can do for her. Usually she will tell me what the issue is but if she doesn't, I will ask her if her hours are working for her, if she would like to talk to a counselor that our company offers, or suggest FMLA until the issue is resolved. Being a leader means to keep a pulse on the group that you are leading and to notice outliers. Bosses must examine sudden changes in behavior. I try to save every employee. It isn't always possible, but everyone deserves a chance.

Treating Everyone Fairly Doesn't Mean Treating Everyone the Same

It helps me to know if my employee is a single parent, going through a divorce, dealing with an illness, going to school while working, or facing any of life's challenges. It helps me to know what hours might work best for them, what days they need off, what weekends they have their kids, and what weekends they can work. To deal effectively with each employee, I've found that his or her current position in life is only part of the story; I also needed to know what type of personality traits he or she possesses.

Although I am friendly with everyone at work—we talk about things that we do on our days off—I don't attend parties at anyone's house or hang out outside of work. This way, I am always fair. I don't attend one party and miss another. I am not favoring one employee over another. In addition, I don't want people to feel uncomfortable because "the boss is there" at an outside activity. As a manager, one cannot party with an employee one day and then coach her the next day when she has done something incorrectly. Therefore, I keep my work life and my personal life separate.

THE WOLF IN SHEEP'S CLOTHING

This is a dangerous employee. She will interview well. During training, she will play the game as if she understands everything. Once she must perform on her own, however, she will not meet the standard. She can be one of many types.

One is the person who keeps a job long enough so that if she is fired, she will get unemployment. Another type will find a reason to go on disability. There are valid reasons for people to be on disability, and we are fortunate that we have that option in our country. But some people use the system. The most dangerous type of wolf, however, is the person who comes on board and immediately starts to look for a reason to sue you. She will find the slightest infraction and go after you. It is unfortunate that these people generally aren't discovered until it is too late, but there are a few warning signs.

Since their goal is avoiding work, they never truly engage with the staff. They may have many absences, keep their personal life very private, or completely isolate themselves during breaks and lunch. They don't want to make friends. They don't want to have connections that make it difficult to walk away. Some people like to keep their professional and home lives separate, but wolves are extremists. They can appear aloof or even arrogant. They have a game plan and are just going through the motions of being an engaged employee. All you can do is stick to the rules. If a wolf steps outside of the rules, treat her like anyone else who breaks the rules. As a manager, you must not only keep your eyes and ears open but also listen to your gut feelings. The wolf may stick around for a couple of years but eventually she will move on. Working long-term is not her goal. She doesn't like how things are managed so she may want to move up so things can be done her way but she doesn't possess the leadership skills to be in a management position. Wolves may engage employees to find fault with a supervisor and make that supervisor miserable until she steps down or quits. The head of the pack will then apply for that position. Never turn your back on a wolf.

The Wolf in Sheep's Clothing in Leadership

This person is pleasant to you to the extent that you might think of her as a friend but her main goal is to make herself look good. If you or your department does anything to bring negative attention to the organization, you are considered weak and expendable. This person may not stay with the organization very long. Her goal is to observe, get close to mid-mangement and then cut positions to save money for the company and to only have people working for her who are aligned with her.

It is all about the numbers to her. She wants to look good on paper no matter what it takes. She is building her resume while in your organization and you may be merely a notch on her belt. Her goal is to move up the corporate ladder. You have options: conform and hopefully wait for her to leave or move on to another organization and hope she doesn't follow you. If conforming means that you have to do things that you consider morally wrong, then you have no option other than to leave.

The Best Day at Work

Leaders would like their departments or companies to run like well-oiled machines—at least on most days. That machine would run something like this. The German shepherds are policing the area to make sure that all tasks are completed quickly and efficiently. The Jack Russells and Australian shepherds are completing the tasks. The Poodles are out on the road selling products or acting as liaisons for the company. The beagles are working on a single account or task, gathering information and sniffing out possibilities. The Chow Chows are working but also making jokes and being witty. The Labradors are working contently and being kind to everyone.

If productivity stays at 100 percent and there are no problems, everyone feels that he or she put in a good day's work for a good day's pay. When the productivity either increases (productivity may be over 100 percent if someone calls in and the same amount of work has to be completed) or decreases substantially, the well-oiled machine starts to break down. Since companies cannot staff for the busiest time every day, except maybe during Christmas or a planned event, the workday can be too busy or too slow. Employees can become overwhelmed or bored.

Not the Best Day at Work

A situation in which employees have too much time on their hands (paws) would look like this. The Australian shepherds and Jack Russells are bored, so they are finding things to do that they have not been trained to do and that are outside their job descriptions. The beagles are happy because they can focus on one thing and completely obsess over it, allowing all other tasks to wait. The Chow Chows are gossiping and complaining about the way the company is run. They maintain that the scheduling and staffing are always incorrect. The Labradors have decreased their energy level and have become a bit impatient. They are people-pleasers and there are not enough people around to please. The Poodles are primping and still trying to strut their stuff, but the audience really isn't large enough, so they are discontent. The German shepherds are pacing. They are nervous and jumpy. They try to get the Jack Russells and Australian shepherds back on track but feel that they are chasing their tails.

To get everything under control, the German shepherds decide to send some of the staff home to better disperse the workload and keep control of the situation. The Chow Chows are the first to be sent home.

When it is too busy, there is less gossiping. But the employees still are unhappy. Employees—except for the teacup breeds—want to do a good job. But too much work is stressful. It sets the stage for errors. Even the Labradors can become nippy under these circumstances. Everyone will start barking at each other and tempers will be short. If possible, a boss should call in extra help to balance the workload. Inevitably, however, there will be days when work is overwhelming. Remember that employees have long memories and that this bad day will be forever etched in their minds.

Bad Doggie

Everyone is on a path in life. For whatever reason, your employees have crossed your path and now work for you. Some will stay with you for a long time. Some will stay in an entry-level position while going to school. Perhaps they will work for the organization in other positions if they are good employees. Some employees see the job as a job, not a career. It pays the bills and buys the food, but they really don't care where they work. They are not stellar performers. You were not there during their formative years, so you can't know why they do the things they do. I once had a dog that I got from the pound who was scared to death if I picked up a newspaper. I would never dream of hurting her, but for the whole time that she blessed me with her existence, she remained afraid of newspapers. Employees will react in ways that you never expect. It may be because of something that happened to them in the past. If they are way out of line, you will have to step in, explain the bad behavior, and set the expectation. Unfortunately, more times than not, once the disciplinary process has started, an employee will end up quitting or being terminated. Sometimes an employee may not fit in your organization but her skill set will fit somewhere else and she will be successful. Other times, the employee just isn't ready for the opportunity that you have offered her and she needs to move on. If you are running a call center and you have hired a Poodle that needs to be with people and strut her stuff, she will probably see the job as a stepping-stone to something else. No one has failed; it is just not a good fit.

If an employee shows accountability after a warning and learns from it, you will have an even stronger employee. You cannot hold a grudge against that employee, and she can't hold one against you, or the relationship will not work. With luck, when you say, "No," to your dog, she will learn and stop the undesired behavior. But neither of you should be scarred for life. You both need to move on.

Praise, Praise, Praise

Both the employee and the dog need praise. With a dog, a few kind words and a treat will probably suffice. It is much more complicated with an employee. Some employees do not like public praise, so they may not want to attend a meeting if the purpose is to acknowledge their good work. Some employees want more than verbal praise, such as, "Good job." Your high performers need new praises and treats. Some employees have an innate need to go above and beyond and their reward is the knowledge that they made a difference. You cannot assume that many employees are like this.

As boss, you need to change it up and not always give the same reward. The gift you give will depend on what your company allows. Movie tickets, massage certificates, gift cards, and free lunches are usually acceptable. Other ways to thank employees are to send thank-you cards to their homes, give a monetary reward (this will probably have to be taxed, so beware), or send flowers. The reward has to match the behavior. The entitled employees would like a reward simply for coming to work. If they see someone else getting a reward, they can become resentful even though they haven't done something to deserve a reward. Many people don't view themselves as others view them. This is why feedback and evaluations are so critical.

Evaluations

Yearly evaluations are mandatory in a successful company, but managers must continually let employees know how they are doing. Yearly evaluations must have certain standards built into them for work habits such as attendance, punctuality, accuracy, and the company's other requirements. If turnaround times are important, address them in both the job description and the evaluation. Whatever is important to the company must be monitored and included in the evaluation. This includes personal behaviors, such as getting along with other employees, representing the company in a positive manner, and being a team player. Be specific. If the employee is not meeting a goal, state exactly what the current behavior is and what the desired behavior should be. Evaluations should never contain surprises. If an employee is not meeting an expectation, this discussion should take place long before the evaluation is given.

On the other hand, if the employee receives an outstanding evaluation, she should have been receiving praise and rewards throughout the year. Take the blinders off while doing the evaluation. Hardly anyone is perfect in every aspect of the job and even the lowest performer has some positive attributes. Consistently reward your high performers. Try to motivate your medium performers to be high performers. Move your low performers up to at least the medium performance level or encourage them to take their skills elsewhere.

Pure Breeds, Mixed Breeds, and Training

Some of our employees are college-educated while some come to us with different backgrounds. In other words, we don't get them as puppies. They have established some traits that we cannot change. Most employees can learn a technical skill, but when laziness or insecurities enter the picture, the employee may not be able to demonstrate the skill. The biggest issue usually is not the skill set but the behavior. Personalities cannot be changed, but one would hope that outward behavior could. This isn't always the case, however. Once an employee has been disciplined or coached for behavioral issues, it is usually his first step toward leaving the organization, either by his choice or by yours. Some employees will see the writing on the wall and leave as soon as they receive a correction from their manager. Other employees will hang in there until the boss actually fires them.

If a dog has a behavior that is not good around children, you do not subject children to that dog. If an employee is not good around customers, you cannot subject customers to that employee. Some people get into a line of work that makes them miserable and instead of looking at themselves and deciding what line of work would make them happy, they complain and make everyone else miserable. With luck, at some point they move on and find an occupation they like. More often than not, however, it is not the occupation that makes them miserable but the fact that they are just unhappy. They will have to make a conscious effort to change their behavior. The first step is to stop being the victim and finger pointing. They must work on themselves. One cannot be a victim and be successful at the same time. Everyone must choose.

So how do you hire the perfect breed? The best employee may be the Heinz 57 variety. They possess (in the correct percentages) the intelligence of a German shepherd, the people skills of the Labrador, and the energy of the Jack Russell. But what are the right percentages? This analysis is tricky, too. If the employee has a highly detailed position, the job may require that she is 75 percent German shepherd. If the job is low on detail and high on people skills, she may have to be 90 percent Labrador. I have never seen "applicant must be a German shepherd" in an ad for a career opportunity, but I would understand it if I did.

What Breed of Dog are You?

By now, you can probably decide which dog type or types match your personality. My husband is a lone wolf. He is not domesticated: He doesn't do chores and he resists routines. He loves doing his own thing. He will start one thing, pick up a new scent, and move to something else. He is very talented and can build anything from an observatory to a car. He doesn't care if I accompany him to an activity; he is happy going alone.

Besides deciding what type of dog you are, it's beneficial to determine how you play with the other dogs. By analyzing your own behavior and that of others, you can get along better with both people and dogs. For example, my husband and I have learned to make our differences work *for* us. Because he is a loner, I am free to write, draw, and pursue my own interests.

The key is to find something good in everyone and realize that we are all social animals and would like to be part of the pack. Move on from there.

What Breed of Dog Do You Own?

You may still be discovering who you are and what type of dog category you fit into, so now is the time to ask what type of dog you own. Does it match your personality? I have owned a Kerry blue terrier, a German shepherd, an Australian shepherd, a golden retriever, a Shih Tzu, an Airedale, and now own a sweet spitz that is seventeen years old. I didn't pick the breeds to match my personality, as many times, I was asked to take in a dog—and, of course, I couldn't say no. My spitz has been the friendliest, happiest dog that I have owned. My mother-in-law didn't want her anymore, so she became my dog. She can be trusted around young children but in her younger years, she killed many rabbits and birds. Now that she is in her retirement years, she stores up her energy until she sees my car approach the house and then runs all around the yard and goes in and out of the doggie door waiting for me to enter the house through the garage. What a nice welcome.

What Breed of Dog is the Author?

I used to be a Jack Russell on steroids when I was a single mother, worked full time, and homeschooled my children. I also had Labrador tendencies, since I wanted everyone to like me. As I have gotten older and, I hope, wiser, I have become a better trained and more focused Jack Russell. I still have many interests and ambitions and sometimes cannot sleep because I have too many things that I am working out in my brain. I am more self-confident than I was when I was younger.

Being a boss made me grow in many ways. I am a director over eighty employees in a hospital currently but have been in management positions over twenty years. The most important way that I have grown is that I have lost some of my people-pleasing needs. I will do anything to help an employee but I know that some people just don't like me, and that is OK. That wasn't OK years ago. I put everyone else before me. I was afraid to stick up for myself or say, "No," fearing that someone might not like me. I no longer compromise my department or myself. If I am invited to an activity that I know I will distain, I will not go. I don't even make excuses. Invite me to go tubing down the river and you may get a curled lip. I have gone tubing. I know it's not for me. It is very crowded, everyone is loud and drinking, and no one has anything thought provoking to say. I can think of hundreds of things that I would rather do—among them, sticking pins in my eyes.

At work, I always try to do what is fair. I have known employees who have gone behind my back. After growling to myself for a little while, I try to look at the situation from their perspective, realizing that neither of us knows the whole picture. Then I try to fix the situation as best I can and move on.

The longer I live, the more aware I am that I don't know everything and the more I study everything and everyone around me. For now, I continue to grow and discover. Sometimes it's painful and sometimes it's exciting. Perhaps my goal should be to transform myself into a cat and be content to watch the world around me. But until then, putting people into different dog categories is not only amusing, but it helps me to cope and accept those who are different from me.

Printed in Great Britain
by Amazon